Every Body's Talking

WHAT WE SAY WITHOUT WORDS

Donna M. Jackson
with Carol Kinsey Goman, PhD

TWENTY-FIRST CENTURY BOOKS / MINNEAPOLIS

With love to Lynn Marie, "Wiggle, wiggle, wiggle!"

Acknowledgments: Many thanks and a hug of appreciation to Carol Kinsey Goman for partnering with me on this book and graciously sharing her knowledge of nonverbal communications. Her input has been invaluable. I'm also deeply grateful to Norine Dresser, Cara Hale Alter, Kalista Consol, Maureen Grier, Pontus Leander, and Lorraine Chasse and family for sharing their insights and experiences for the book.

A special note of thanks and gratitude to Domenica Di Piazza for her generous guidance and editorial expertise. Her enthusiasm for this book from the start helped make all the difference. Thanks also to the ultra-creative photo, design, and production teams at Lerner, and to Susan Cohen at Writers House for her literary direction. Most of all, thanks to Charlie "Papa" Jackson, who eyes every word with love. You're the best.

A portion of the proceeds from this book has been donated by the authors to Promises2Kids, an organization that reaches out with loving arms to help hurting kids heal.

Twenty-First Century Books
A division of Lerner Publishing Group, Inc.
241 First Avenue North
Minneapolis, MN 55401 U.S.A.

For reading levels and more information, look up this title at www.lernerbooks.com

Library of Congress Cataloging-in-Publication Data

Jackson, Donna M., 1959–
     Every body's talking : what we say without words / by Donna M. Jackson.
        page   cm.
     Includes bibliographical references and index.
     ISBN 978–1–4677–0858–6 (lib. bdg. : alk. paper)
     ISBN 978–1–4677–1120–3 (eBook)
     1. Body language—Juvenile literature. 2. Nonverbal communication—Juvenile literature. I. Title.
     BF637.N66J33 2014
     153.6'9—dc23   2013019674

Manufactured in the United States of America
1 – DP – 12/31/13

Contents

The way we move our bodies and the expressions we make with our facial muscles and our eyes are powerful signals for communicating feelings and thoughts.

1

LOUDER THAN WORDS

You could see it in their eyes and hands and feet. It was the teens' first performance on stage. One girl's fingers trembled as she cradled her guitar. The other clung to her microphone. Though their harmonies sparkled, the pair's voices trickled out in a whisper. No worries. People in the audience leaned in to listen. They understood the telltale signs of stage fright.

Like the nervous teens, we're always talking—with our words and with our actions. Scientists say more than half our communication is conveyed nonverbally through body language. From head to toe, our bodies say volumes about our thoughts, attitudes, and feelings—whether we want them to or not. Sometimes we express these messages through gestures. We'll nod our head in agreement or throw our arms up as a sign of victory.

Other times our faces give us away. Someone cuts in line, and our jaw tightens; a friend compliments our eyes, and our cheeks flush. Even our posture—straight or slouched; the way we walk—briskly or slowly; and the amount of space we put between ourselves and others—inches or yards—tell stories.

The conversations begin the moment we're born. Ever watch babies "talk"? They say what they feel without using words. A broad smile beams, "I'm delighted." An eye rub signals, "I'm ready for a nap." Babies are tiny bundles of body language, with each move reflecting their emotions of the moment. This instinctual first language is key to human survival. That's because, as infants, we're totally dependent on others to feed and care for us. Nonverbal signals or cues, such as eye contact and facial expressions, help babies and their parents emotionally attach to each other. These powerful bonds foster a sense of security in infants, who learn to trust their environment. They also motivate parents to love and protect their children around the clock.

YOU DON'T SAY!

To keep discussions polite, the city council in Palo Alto, California, once considered banning rude body language during its political debates. Unwelcome expressions included smirks and eyebrows raised in disbelief. "I don't think the people sitting around the cabinet with the [US] president roll their eyes," said one councilwoman. Ultimately, the plan received a thumbs-down.

The human survival instinct is one reason "we're better at picking up negative signals than positive ones," says Carol Kinsey Goman, a body language expert and author of *The Nonverbal Advantage: Secrets and Science of Body Language at Work.* The emotional center of our brain, a primitive area known as the limbic system, acts as an alarm and immediately alerts us to perceived threats. These threats can be physical or psychological. The moment our brain senses danger, we react. We may freeze in place until the threat passes, flee the situation, or fight back. Whatever we do, the associated emotions show in our body language. Since these reactions are biologically based and happen before we can think, many experts believe they're the most reliable indicators of what people are feeling.

limbic system

spinal cord

The limbic system is a set of brain structures that controls motivation, emotion, learning, and memory.

A similar process occurs for all our emotions. The limbic system reacts to what it sees—something happy or sad, for instance—and then signals the body to express what it feels. This is why it plays a key role in all nonverbal communication.

MULTIPLE EXPRESSIONS

As babies grow into toddlers and begin to talk, messages become more complex. Now we can express ourselves with words *and* actions, either

SOUNDS OF SILENCE

Lights . . . Camera . . . Action! Or maybe not. We've all had "deer in the headlights" moments *(below)*. The teacher calls on us, and we don't know the answer. We're giving a talk, and our mind suddenly goes blank. The emotional center of our brain, our limbic system, reacts instantly to the fear that we'll look foolish. So what happens? We feel trapped, and our survival response is to freeze and clam up. The next time you're in the spotlight and you freeze, move past the moment as quickly as possible. Breathe deeply, smile if you can, and say something—anything related to the topic—to push forward. And as you do, use your hands. Studies show that using hand gestures not only keeps your body from looking stiff, it also helps you find the right words.

alone or at the same time. When the two are in sync, they may complement each other. "Nice job!" we shout to a teammate and follow up with a highfive. Actions like this increase friendship and trust. But when our bodies say one thing and our words another, we send mixed messages that can confuse people and create tension. This happens not only when people lie, but also when they feel nervous or unsure about what they're saying. "Ready for tryouts?" you ask a friend. "Of course!" he says with his words. But his downcast eyes tell another story. And that's the one people are most likely to believe.

A jubilant highfive is a physical expression of happiness and success. Adding a jump signals intensity of emotion.

"Many times, we're unaware that we can look like we're being deceitful, or look like we don't know an answer, or look like we don't want to be there by avoiding eye contact . . ." says Goman. "*How we* say something, and *how* we look when we say it, tells people more about what we're feeling than practically any of the words we use." When we believe what we say, we usually look like we do, says Goman. Problem is, some people are shy, introverted, or not sure that others will believe them. As a result, their body language doesn't always reflect their true feelings. "They let fears or bad habits—such as slouching and finger-tapping—take over their body, so their confidence in their words doesn't come through," explains Goman.

Luckily, we don't need to learn every signal to interpret nonverbal behaviors. So says Joe Navarro, a former intelligence agent with the Federal Bureau of Investigation (FBI). When you look at someone's behavior, he says, ask yourself one question: "Am I seeing comfort or discomfort?" When people are comfortable and relaxed, they take up space by keeping their arms open and gesturing with their hands. They'll smile, lean toward you, and make eye contact. People who send comfort signals are typically saying they're happy in the moment and that they like you or an activity they're engaged in.

On the other hand, when people are uncomfortable, they'll avert their

TAKE ACTION!

Reading body language can be tricky. While the goal is to better understand people, there are plenty of ways to misread them as well. It also takes practice to focus on both words and the body. Start by watching other people's behaviors when you're not involved. This could be in school, at a mall, or in a restaurant. Who looks comfortable and who doesn't? What nonverbal cues give them away?

gaze and "get small." They'll roll in their shoulders and cross their arms and legs. They may also try to calm themselves and work off nervous energy by jiggling their feet or twirling their hair. When people send discomfort signals, they're telling you something's wrong. It could be with you, them, or the situation. Whatever it is, it's making them uneasy.

"These are the very same signals that other people judge you by," notes Goman. When you look comfortable, people think you're engaged and interested.

Twirling hair can be a sign of emotional discomfort. Combined with other physical signs, such as lip biting and small eyes, it probably says a person is nervous and ill at ease. When you pay attention to a group of signs like these, it can help you better understand what another person is saying without words.

When you look uncomfortable, they think you're detached, resistant or bored.

Imagine you've been talking comfortably with a friend for a while. After some time, he suddenly steps back, sighs, and begins glancing at the door. His behaviors are telling you he's uncomfortable and ready to leave. You can ignore the signs and keep talking. Or you can listen to his body language and wrap things up. By ending the conversation, you're showing that you understand his actions and that you respect them as well.

YOU DON'T SAY!

While hair twirling can start out as a way to relieve stress, says Goman, it may also develop into a habit that girls (and women) use even when they're not stressed.

Establishing eye contact—or not—is a critical component of human communication. Direct eye contact, along with a happy smile, is a sure sign of friendship or comfort between two people.

2

HERE'S LOOKING AT YOU

They can sparkle with love or flash in anger. Roll in ridicule or twinkle with joy.

No other facial feature attracts attention and reveals our thoughts more reliably than the eyes. When we're content, they're warm and welcoming. When we're upset, we shield them from the world. The ancient Parintintin Indians of South America viewed eyes as powerful storytellers. For this reason, they ate the eyes of their enemies to keep their ghosts from avenging their deaths.

Our eyes stream more messages than any other part of the body, says Goman. A single glance can convey a range of emotions—from a startled, "Whoa . . . what was that?" to a stinging, "Don't even think about it!" People squint their eyes with suspicion, avert them in guilt, wink them in greeting, and widen them in surprise. In a sense, "we exist behind our eyes," says Daniel McNeill, author of *The Face*. They glow when the mind buzzes. "And when thought and feeling are absent, they can look hard as marbles."

EYE TO EYE

The moment we meet a person's eyes, we establish a relationship. When it's positive, eye contact reflects our interest in and curiosity about the other person and gives us the chance to get to know that person better. As we talk, we make eye contact through a series of steady glances, says Goman. The more we like someone, the longer we tend to look at that person—usually about two-thirds of the time we're together.

Depending on the relationship, our gaze changes. When talking with teachers and other adults, for example, our gaze is businesslike. It is also directed at the upper part of the face, from the eyes up. When talking with people we like socially, our gaze drops toward the mouth. "It becomes more friendly and flirtatious," says Goman.

In Western cultures, eye contact is also a sign of respect. "If you look at someone, they believe you're paying attention," says Goman. "Say, for example, you're in class and the teacher's explaining an assignment. If you let your eyes roam around the room instead of watching her, it *looks* like you're not listening. And that's how she'll judge you—whether or not you've heard every word."

The same applies in sports. "Coaches love to see your eyes," says Dena Evans, director of the Point Guard College basketball training program. Making eye contact helps build trust between a player and a coach, says Evans. When kids walk away or toss the ball back and forth while their coach is talking, she says, it gives the coach the impression that they're not listening or don't care about what's being said. "It sort of feels like it's a waste of your time and energy," she says.

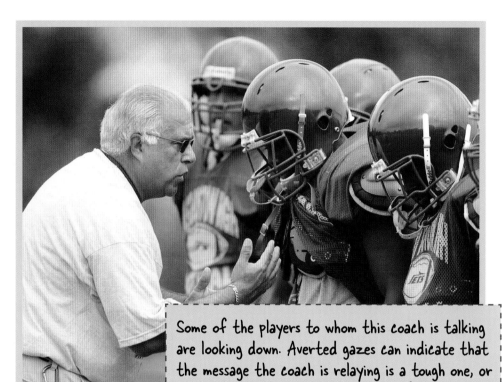

Some of the players to whom this coach is talking are looking down. Averted gazes can indicate that the message the coach is relaying is a tough one, or that the players aren't listening carefully.

EYE-CATCHERS

Our eyes send and receive thousands of nonverbal messages each day. Here are a few key eye moves that communicate our feelings.

BLINKS: Human eyes normally blink about every four seconds, or fifteen times a minute. The rate increases under stress.

DARTING EYES: Eyes that move rapidly without fixing on a specific spot signal heightened emotions. The person may be nervous, defensive, or insecure.

EYE BLOCK: A person may momentarily close, cover, or rub the eyes. This indicates that the person is upset or thinking about something.

EYEBROW FLASH: The quick lifting and lowering of the eyebrows is a sign of recognition and greeting.

EYE ROLL: This disrespectful move shows doubt or lack of interest in what another person is saying.

PUPILLOMETRICS

One study found that we judge people as more physically attractive if they're looking directly at us and smiling. It's our way of deciding whether they like us. If they do, we, in turn, find *them* more likable. Another way to gauge someone's interest is to apply pupillometrics and check the size of the person's pupils. When we like someone or something, our pupils dilate, or enlarge. When we don't like what we see, they constrict. Looking at someone's pupils can give you a sense of how well a conversation may be going. Just be sure the person is reacting to you and not to an object in the background. Pupil size can change when a person is looking at a cute classmate . . . or at a chocolate pie.

FLASHBULB EYES: An exaggerated opening of the eyes (*above*), this movement indicates intense fear or anger.
HAIRY EYEBALL: A lowered upper eyelid typically means disapproval.
LOWERED GAZE: This move can signal respect for authority, embarrassment, or submissiveness.
SIDEWAYS GLANCE: If accompanied by a smile and raised eyebrows, looking off to the side can be a sign of interest. However, if the gaze goes along with a downturned mouth and lowered eyebrows, it can be an unfriendly, critical, or suspicious signal.

MORE THAN MEETS THE EYE

In general, the greater the eye contact between two people, the more it leads to liking. That is, unless the eye contact becomes a stare or a glare. "A stare is extended eye contact that doesn't break. A glare is when you harden your eyes around that stare so that your eyelids get harder," says Goman. "Both are signs of challenge and aggression that we pick up on long before anybody says a word."

Lack of eye contact is also unsettling. It's almost impossible to connect with someone who doesn't look at you. Think back to a time when you didn't want the teacher to call on you in class. "You probably looked down and pretended to take notes," says Goman. "Intuitively, you knew that if you looked up, it would say you were engaged and paying attention." And that's the last signal you wanted to send.

People avoid eye contact for many reasons. They may be shy, sad, insecure, embarrassed, depressed, uninterested, or lying. (In some cases, though, a liar will have no problem looking you in the eye, and truth-tellers may avoid your gaze.) It's also difficult to make or maintain eye contact with someone when you're angry or talking about sensitive issues.

TAKE ACTION!

One way to increase eye contact and to build relationships is to look at people's eyes long enough to notice their color. Try this with at least one person a day. See if you notice a difference in the way people respond to you.

No matter what the reason, avoiding eye contact makes others uncomfortable. We tend to associate it with being impolite, bored, distracted, or distrustful. It can be a problem when going through security at airports, too. Behavior detection officers look twice at people who act nervous and avoid eye contact. For example, at the airport in Miami, Florida, two security officers noticed a young woman trying to hide her face at a security checkpoint. They pulled her aside. Turns out, the people she was traveling with had beaten and kidnapped her. Police promptly arrested them.

Hiding the face and eyes is one way to signal insecurity or fear.

Cartoonists pay special attention to body language and emphasize it in their work to humorous effect.

3

BODIES IN MOTION

When actor Maureen Grier prepares for a role, she dives into it—head to toe. Whether she's playing a doctor or a nun or a gym teacher, she starts by "hanging out with people for a while, just to get a sense of how they function in the world," she says. "I watch the way they move and listen to how they talk." Sometimes she'll even look in the mirror and make faces to practice different emotions. "You feel it, and you see what it looks like," she says. "Then your body will have a muscle memory to draw on when you need it."

Actors performing roles, police officers tracking criminals, and artists creating characters all use body language skills at work. In *How to Draw Funny*, for example, the authors show how to add emotions to "dull doodles" to make them comical. Happy characters, they say, look like they're "floating on air," with arms, eyebrows, and feet all pointing up.

Figures in pain clench their bodies. They close their eyes, grit their teeth, and squeeze their shoulders all the way up to their ears.

KINESICS

Kinesics is the scientific study of body movements and their role in communication. By watching people's actions—how they hold their bodies and walk into a room—we can pick up information about how they may be feeling at the moment.

POSTURE

One quick way to read body language is to look at people's posture—how they sit and stand. Open posture is relaxed, receptive, and typically front-facing. Arms and legs are unfolded, and the palms of the hands face up or hang loosely at the sides. Closed posture looks tight and often suggests disagreement or discomfort. Arms and legs are crossed, and the body is turned away from other people. Not surprisingly, open posture is viewed as more positive and persuasive. One study even found that when people sit with their arms and legs uncrossed, it improves their memory.

STANCES

"The closer you put your feet together, the more you look like a pushover," says Goman. "Because literally, you are." When people widen their stance by placing their feet about shoulder distance apart, it's physically more difficult to knock them off balance or push them over. So when you widen your stance, you look more grounded and more confident.

WALKING STYLE

We make many decisions about people based on the way they walk, says Goman. If they walk slowly and look at the ground, we view them as depressed or even lazy. "If they have good posture and walk briskly, we believe they have someplace to go and something to do." The next time you have to get up in front of the class, pull your shoulders back and walk briskly to the front of the room, she advises. "You'll look—and feel—more confident," even before you open your mouth!

BODY ANGLING

The more positive you feel about someone, the more you tend to angle your body toward that person. That's especially true if the person has status or rank. You show respect by orienting your body toward the high-ranking person. On the other hand, if you turn your head toward someone but leave your shoulders and stomach pointed the other way, you're not giving the person your full attention, says Goman. This indicates that you're probably not very interested in them or what they have to say.

PROXEMICS

The way we use personal space, called proxemics, sends many unspoken messages. One includes how close we feel to other people. In general, the more we know and trust someone, the less space we need between us. While we have no problem standing close enough to hug our parents, we'll probably keep a social distance of 4 to 12 feet (1.2 to 3.7 meters)

MIRROR, MIRROR

One way to let people know you like or agree with them is to mirror their positive body language. It's something we do naturally when we talk with our best friends. If they tilt their heads to the right, we tilt our heads to the left. If they lean forward, we lean forward. Sometimes, we even unconsciously match their voice volume and breathing rates.

"Mirroring is part of looking friendly and warm and interested in the person that you're talking with," says Goman. "As a technique, you want to wait a few seconds after the person takes a posture before reflecting it." Then you want to mirror it slowly and subtly. "If you mimic the behavior too soon, they'll catch it and think you're making fun of them," she says. "But if you do it right, it's a very positive thing. It's positive with parents, teachers, and the people you want to impress." When you notice that people mirror *your* moves, you'll know you're on the same wavelength.

when talking with a clerk at a store. We also judge other people's relationships by the amount of space they put between themselves. "If we see someone whispering in another person's ear *[like the two girls at left]*, we figure they must be good friends, because they're standing so close," says Goman. "You don't just let anyone do that."

FACIAL EXPRESSIONS

Our faces express emotions faster and more effectively than words. Of the ten thousand or so expressions scientists estimate we can make, only seven are recognized across cultures. These are:

HAPPINESS: A true smile of enjoyment is easy to spot, says Dr. Paul Ekman, a leading researcher of facial expressions. It happens spontaneously and engages the muscles of the mouth and eyes. With a true smile, our cheeks lift and our faces seem to light up. Other smiles, like the polite smile we make when taking school photos, use only the muscles around the mouth.

SADNESS: When we lose something, such as a game, a pet, or even a person's trust, we look and feel sad. Our upper eyelids droop, and the corners of our mouths curl down.

ANGER: When someone intentionally hurts us, we feel a sense of injustice and become angry. Our eyes glare, our lips narrow, and our eyebrows angle down to form a *V*.

FEAR: A survival instinct, fear helps us stay safe in dangerous situations. When we're afraid, our eyebrows lift and pull together, our lower eyelids tense, and our lips stretch back in a straight line toward the ears.

Tight body language, along with downcast eyes and lips, communicates sadness or depression.

DISGUST: Slimy worms and cruel people: both can repulse us and make our faces pucker with wrinkled noses and elevated upper lips.

CONTEMPT: People who feel contempt for someone feel morally superior on some level. They think, *I would never do that!* The result is a scornful sneer—an expression that tightens and raises the lip corner on one side of the face.

SURPRISE: When we're surprised, our eyes widen, the eyebrows lift, and our mouths open. This feeling only lasts a few seconds, until we figure out what's happening.

Each of these emotions can vary in intensity and show on people's faces to different degrees. All are innate. Researchers know this because they appear on the faces of children who have been blind since birth. When people try to hide their true emotions, they can leak out in micro-expressions. These fleeting facial expressions last less than one-fifth of a second and are difficult to spot. If you see one, however, it may reveal how your friend really feels about an upcoming move.

ALL SMILES

Along with the true smile of happiness, we make many other smiles. There's the embarrassed smile, where we look down or off to the side so we don't meet a person's eyes. There's the flirtatious smile, where we quickly steal a sideways glance at the person of interest. And then there's the miserable smile, where we press our lips together tightly to grin and bear whatever's in front of us.

When someone fakes a smile, it's often asymmetrical—more pronounced on one side of the face than the other. It also excludes the eye muscles. Real or not, smiling has been found to relieve stress, lift our mood, and make difficult tasks seem easier. One Russian Olympic weight-training coach urged his athletes to smile when lifting weights and discovered it improved their performance.

TAKE ACTION!

Smile at five people today and notice how many mirror back your friendly gesture.

SHOULDERS

Shoulders may look quiet, but they say a lot. When they're loose and at ease, a person is comfortable and feeling safe. When they swing from side to side, the person may be moving to music or feeling generally happy. If we hold them back, it's a sign of confidence. If we turn them away from

The turtle move—burying the head in the shoulders—is a classic sign of fear and insecurity. So are this girl's awkward smile and her overly busy hands.

24

someone, we're giving him the cold shoulder. When someone's insecure, she may shrug her shoulders and bury her head in her neck like a turtle.

Taken alone, shoulder shrugs say, *I don't know, I don't care,* or *I don't understand.* When people say something definitive but shrug their shoulders, they lose credibility, says Goman. "You've said with your body, 'I don't really know what I'm talking about,' or 'I don't really believe what I'm talking about,' or 'I'm unsure.' "

TORSO

Follow the belly button. That's what body language expert Janine Driver does to measure someone's interest. If it's pointing in your direction, she says, you have that person's attention. When we like someone, we also tend to lean in slightly with our torso to encourage that person to keep talking. If we don't like a person or an object, we may lean back to distance ourselves.

When people feel defensive, they'll cross their arms or use items such as books to cover their upper body. It's probably an unconscious way of protecting themselves, says Goman. The tighter the grip on the item, the more discomfort the person is probably feeling.

HELPING HANDS

Hand gestures are a natural part of our communication. Talking without them is incredibly difficult. In fact, we use our hands when we're talking on the phone, even though we know the other person can't see us. One reason talking and hand gestures are so closely linked is that they're processed in the same regions of the brain—Broca's area and Wernicke's area.

Gesturing has also been found to help children to learn new words, to solve visualization problems (such as picturing an object from different angles), and to remember new material longer. Just watching people talk with their hands has been found to improve learning.

Hands not only help us learn, they can also replace, strengthen, or accent our words. When we put a finger to our lips, we're saying, "Be quiet!" When we point as we declare, "It's behind the chair," we reinforce our message. And when we clench a fist while telling someone to stay away, we amplify our threat.

Since hands say so many things, we tend to distrust people who hide them in their pockets or under a table. We feel more comfortable when we can see a person's open palms, which is a signal of trust and acceptance.

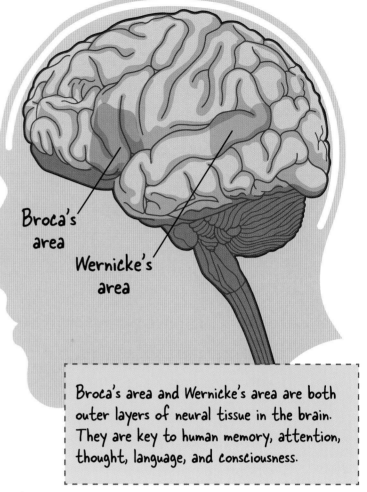

Broca's area

Wernicke's area

Broca's area and Wernicke's area are both outer layers of neural tissue in the brain. They are key to human memory, attention, thought, language, and consciousness.

THE POWER OF TOUCH

Need something from a parent? Reach out and touch them—on their arm, shoulder, or hand, says Goman. Studies show that if you touch someone, they'll be more likely to grant you a favor. This is one reason waiters and waitresses briefly touch customers. They know odds are they'll get a bigger tip.

The study of touch as nonverbal communication is called haptics. Researchers are finding that little touches may reap big rewards. Scientists at the University of California–Berkeley analyzed "every bump, hug, and high five in a single game played by each team in the National Basketball Association" and found overall that the teams and players who touched most performed best.

According to research, players who hug are likely to perform better than those who don't touch each other at all during a game.

FANCY FOOTWORK

If you're looking for the truth, watch people's feet. They're the farthest from the brain and the least likely to be consciously controlled. "We don't train our feet to hide feelings the way we train our faces, so they're often the most accurate signals [of true feeling]," says Goman. Much like our eyes and belly buttons, our feet tend to point toward people and objects we like or toward places we want to go.

"Feet will also reach out and touch you if they like you," says Goman. Couples who are dating often touch feet under the table. When someone is feeling left out of a conversation, he may pull his feet under his chair.

Fidgety feet often suggest boredom and impatience, especially for men and boys. People also bounce, kick, jiggle, tap, shuffle, or rock their feet to relieve stress when they're nervous. In contrast, happy feet jump for joy. They're usually attached to lucky soles waiting in line for ice cream or amusement park rides.

Feet often reveal our true feelings, as in the case of these two people playing footsie underneath a table.

YOU DON'T SAY!

Not sure if you should join a conversation between two friends? Look at their feet. If they turn the foot nearest you in your direction, you're welcome to join in. If their torsos turn and their feet stay put, it's a private conversation that's best not to interrupt.

VOICE MESSAGES

Our voices send nonverbal cues too. Voices reveal our feelings and can change the meaning of our messages. These vocal cues are expressed in the way we deliver our words—such as our tone of voice and whether it is friendly, supportive, or teasing—and by how quickly we talk. Angry messages, for example, are often sent in voices that are loud, high pitched, and fast paced. Loving messages, on the other hand, are usually delivered in soft, low-pitched, relaxed voices. Vocal cues also help us to emphasize particular points and to let people know whether we're asking a question, making a statement, or giving a command. Even our ums, ahs, likes, and you knows send a message. If we use them too often, they convey doubt and make us sound less believable.

TAKE ACTION!

When under stress, your vocal pitch rises, says Goman. "A good trick before you speak is to put your lips together and say "Um Hm" three times. This brings your voice down into its optimum pitch."

Signs of discomfort such as tight body language and an insincere smile can indicate fear. They can also tell you that a person is lying.

4

SPOTTING LIES

Leave me alone. Everything's fine.
I finished my homework at school.
What? I didn't take that last cookie!

Spotting a lie isn't always this easy. Most times people aren't so obvious. That is, unless like preschoolers, they're new to fibbing. Younger children tend to give away their guilt by covering their mouths, hiding their hands behind their backs, and nervously trying to squirm their way out of a situation. As they grow older, they develop more sophisticated methods that are more difficult to recognize.

Unless a person confesses or we catch that person in a lie, it's pretty hard to know whether or not someone's lying to us. "There is no such thing as a human lie detector," say the former Central Intelligence Agency officers who wrote the book *Spy the Lie*. However, there are ways to pick up signs of deception—not only in someone's words, but in their body language too.

YOU DON'T SAY!

Creepy people can give us the chills—literally making us feel physically colder—say researchers at the University of Groningen in the Netherlands. When someone acts friendly, for example, but doesn't mimic our moves the way we would expect a friendly person to do, it leaves us feeling cold. "You can feel in your gut that [the odd body language is] not a good thing," says study coauthor, Pontus Leander.

"When you lie, your brain has to work overtime, and that causes stress," says Goman. One study at Temple University in Pennsylvania found that more areas of the brain activate when people tell lies than when they tell the truth. This includes the prefrontal cortex, a region of the brain responsible for decisionmaking. Researchers believe the increased activity reflects the extra work our brains do in deciding to lie and then in thinking up a story. Most people who tell a lie also feel some discomfort. The bigger the lie, the more uncomfortable they may feel and the more worried they may be about getting caught. All this tension leaks out in a person's behaviors.

TO TELL THE TRUTH

Let's say you ask a friend to help you clean your room. "Help you clean your room?" she says, shaking her head side to side. "I'd really like to, but I need to stop at home and feed the dogs first. Sorry," she says, shrugging her shoulders and flashing a little smile.

How can you tell if you should believe her?

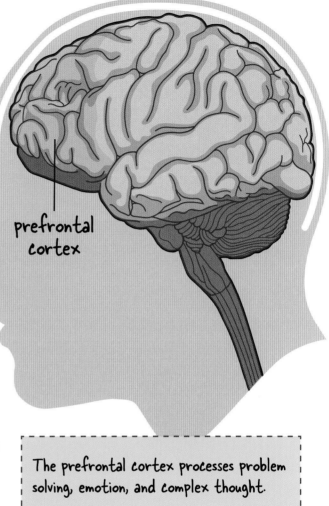

prefrontal cortex

The prefrontal cortex processes problem solving, emotion, and complex thought.

CLUE #1: She repeated your question before answering it. Unless your friend usually responds this way, she may have been stalling to think of a reason to get out of helping you.

CLUE #2: She sent mixed signals—shaking her head no while saying that she'd really like to help. When people's gestures don't match their words, pay attention. Our brains and bodies normally work together when we're telling the truth.

CLUE #3: After turning down your request, your friend shrugged her shoulders—a sign of uncertainty—and smiled briefly. This out-of-context grin could be Duper's Delight, the fleeting smile that people make when they're inwardly tickled about fooling someone.

Given the situation, your friend may be uncomfortable telling you she can't help. Or she may act this way in general. The key is in the timing of her response. The first sign of deception (pausing) came right away. If this was the only suspicious sign, you would be pretty safe believing your friend's explanation. But you've spotted a cluster of signals—two or more potentially misleading behaviors. The more signs you identify, the more confident you can be about spotting a lie.

Even with a cluster of clues, however, you can't be 100 percent sure that your friend is lying. You'll have to ask more questions if you really want to know. Depending on your relationship, these can be anything from a blunt "Seriously? Are you telling me the truth?" to a more diplomatic "Maybe I'm wrong, but do you really need to go home, or was it rude of me to ask you to clean?" If your friend is lying, your follow-up questions may persuade her to tell you the truth. If that doesn't work, you might want to let it go. It may not be worth hurting your friendship over this issue.

HALO OR DEVIL'S HORNS?

"The more you know someone, the easier it is to tell if he's lying, because you have a baseline," says Goman. You notice when your sister's lip biting may be a sign of a lie, based on how typical it is of her overall behavior. "The only time familiarity gets in the way is when you like or

SIGNS OF DECEPTION

Spotting lies isn't an exact science, but there are clues to look for that help. To increase your chances of detecting a lie, watch for a cluster of cues that signal uneasiness or discomfort. These may include:

MOUTH COVERING: If you ask someone a question, and she reaches to cover some part of her face *(right)* with a hand—especially the mouth or cheek—take note. It could mean something's up.

NOSE TOUCHING: Scientists have found that the area around our nose heats up when we lie. This is called the Pinocchio effect, after the storybook character whose

love someone so much that you can't see when they're lying," continues Goman. The halo effect means we have positive feelings about someone in all areas, based on a single good trait or on how much we like or love that person. The opposite is the devil's horns—having negative feelings about someone overall, based on a negative characteristic and/or how much we dislike that person.

But what if you don't know the person well? What if it's someone you've just met? How can you gain a sense of whether or not you can nose grew longer with each lie. Some people find themselves lightly rubbing, touching, or scratching their itchy, tingly noses as they get ready to tell a lie.

PACIFYING GESTURES: When people are under stress, they soothe themselves by touching parts of their body. They may rub their legs, wring their hands, massage between their eyes, or hug themselves by wrapping their arms across the chest.

GROOMING GESTURES: Another way people release nervous energy is by making themselves look good and tidying their surroundings. If someone suddenly starts adjusting his cap, fixing his hair, or organizing his locker as he's answering a question, he may be uneasy with the question. He may also be lying to you.

LEANING AWAY: When someone is uncomfortable with something she just said, such as a lie, she may try to physically distance herself from you by leaning back her head and torso. This also reduces her emotional connection to you.

UNUSUAL STILLNESS: Some people keep abnormally still when they're lying as a way to avoid giving out cues. But in fact, if someone suddenly freezes like a statue for no obvious reason, that's a cue. She may be lying and is working really hard to avoid sending untrustworthy signals.

trust that person? One study used college students and a social robot named Nexi to find out. The goal was to identify gestures that were most likely to predict an untrustworthy person—or robot. Researchers at Northeastern University, the Massachusetts Institute of Technology, and Cornell University conducted two experiments. In the first one, students briefly introduced themselves to each other. Then they played a game involving tokens and trust. In the second experiment, students introduced themselves to Nexi (who did likewise) and played the same game with the robot. Scientists found that four gestures—when clustered together—were especially accurate at predicting dishonest behaviors. These gestures were face touching, hand touching, leaning away, and crossing arms over the chest. This group of gestures triggered similar feelings of distrust, whether they

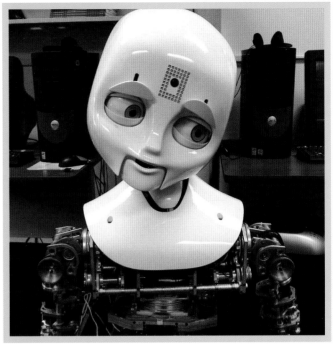

SOCIAL ROBOTS

Imagine having a robot as one of your best friends. It may be possible someday. Scientists are working to create machines that not only think logically but can also express emotions through common gestures and facial expressions. Turns out, people respond subconsciously to a robot's social cues in much the same way they react to human body language. "A robot, simply by the way it makes eye contact with you, can impact how trustworthy you perceive it to be," says Cynthia Breazeal, director of the Personal Robots Group at the media lab at the Massachusetts Institute of Technology. Breazeal has developed several socially savvy robots, including Kismet, Leonardo, and Nexi. She envisions a future where machines that understand body language will work with people in their daily lives.

One charming robot that's already teaming up with people is Keepon. It was designed to help autistic children, who often have difficulty forming relationships and communicating face to face. Keepon is yellow and shaped like a snowman. It has two cameras for eyes and a microphone nose. Its creator, came from a person or from Nexi. It seems we're hard wired to connect certain behaviors to intentions, says Professor Robert H. Frank, one of the authors of the study. "When we see [a body cue], whether it's a robot or a human, we're affected by it, because of the pattern it evokes in our brain responses."

Nexi (opposite page) and Keepon (right) are social robots that mimic some human movements, gestures, and expressions.

Hideki Kozima at Miyagi University in Japan, purposely built the robot with simple features and movements. This way, an autistic child would feel comfortable interacting with it.

The plan worked. Keepon's cute face and straightforward responses—it nods, rocks, turns, and bobs—charm autistic children. Over time, they make eye contact with the robot and even touch, nurture, and protect it from other children.

A few years after Keepon was created, Marek Michalowski, a roboticist from San Francisco, California, added dancing to the robot's talents. Keepon now bobs rhythmically to upbeat tempos and sways to slow ones. The robot also became a star on YouTube dancing to hit songs. You can even buy a simplified version of the robot, called My Keepon, for less than fifty dollars!

Light kissing of the cheeks is a common greeting or farewell among friends in many parts of the world.

5

MULTICULTURAL MOVES

College freshman Kalista Consol knows what it's like to study overseas. She visited fourteen countries in three months and experienced new worlds of body language. In Spain she saw people greet each other with cheek kisses and hugs. In England it was a proper handshake. But the most charming welcome she witnessed—and shared—was in the African nation of Ghana.

"From the second I stepped off the ship, people were giving me friendly hugs and were quick to call me sister," she says. "They treated all of us as if we had known each other for a while." Most impressive was the Ghanaian handshake. "At the start of talking to anyone, you would grab hands as if shaking them, and then while continuing to hold hands, you'd take your thumb and middle finger and snap once or twice," she says. "If you really wanted to be swag about it, you would double snap—rolling one snap off your middle finger into another with your index finger."

Many times, Ghanaians would continue to hold hands throughout their conversation or grab them again to repeat the snaps. "Any number of things could cause you to snap again," says Consol. "You might get excited about the subject, or about meeting people, or making plans. You might even snap if they agree with what you're saying, or if you just want to reaffirm the connection between the two of you." The greeting

A Ghanaian handshake includes snapping of the enlaced fingers of two people who are greeting each other.

symbolized the Ghanaian culture. "People were so quick to connect with you . . . they were energetic, extroverted, and passionate about life. Every interaction seemed to involve lots of smiles."

As Consol discovered, the Ghanaians are a contact culture, where people frequently use touch to communicate. During conversations they may spontaneously wrap an arm around the person they're talking to, squeeze his shoulder, or touch her wrist. "These gestures show trust or

GLOBAL GESTURES

Our gestures are more likely to be misread across cultures than anything we say in words. One reason is that many common moves carry different meanings across the globe. What's friendly in one country may be insulting in another. When traveling, be on the lookout for these cultural differences. You can also learn more about the country you'll be visiting by checking online or in a guidebook.

NODDING in the United States means "yes." In Albania and Bulgaria, it means "no."

The **OK SIGN** means "all is well" in North America and "zero" in Australia. In Japan it is a symbol for money. But in Brazil, Mexico, and Turkey, it's an insult. And in Kuwait, it's the sign for the "evil eye," a curse.

CROSSING FINGERS is a way people in the United States, Scandinavia, and the United Kingdom ask for good luck. In fact, in the United Kingdom, it's the logo for the national lottery. But don't use it in Vietnam, where it represents female body parts and is highly offensive.

SLURPING may be impolite in Western cultures, but it is considered good table approval," says Goman. The potential for misunderstanding comes when people from contact cultures, such as Greece, Israel, Saudi Arabia, and most of Latin America, meet people from noncontact cultures. These include Germany, Japan, Britain, Canada, and the United States. On the one hand, people who value touch in relationships may be offended when someone doesn't return the touch. On the other hand, people who prefer very little contact may feel uneasy being showered with touches.

manners when you're eating noodles or drinking tea in Japan. Refined slurps (not sloppy ones) tell everyone you're enjoying your meal.

SHOWING THE SOLES OF YOUR SHOES is a serious insult in Egypt and in Arab cultures. That's because the bottoms of shoes become soiled. Baring them to others is like comparing the other person to dirt.

THUMBS-UP translates to approval in the United States. In Italy it means "one," in Japan it means "five," and in Greece it's a rude gesture that's similar to flipping the bird.

CLOSE CALLS

Differences in personal space can add to the cultural confusion. For example, Americans typically prefer a social distance of 4 to 7 feet (1.2 to 2.1 meters) when meeting someone new. Many other cultures favor half that or less. "The personal space bubble was much smaller in Ghana," says Consol, who admits she was a little overwhelmed at first. "Many of my friends felt the Ghanaians were rude because they stood so close and felt so free to grab our hands. However, we started to adjust by the end of our stay and understood it was a cultural thing."

It's important to take culture into consideration when someone's body language is different or seems off, says Norine Dresser, a folklorist and author of *Multicultural Manners*. "People can misread cues, which may lead to bad feelings." Dresser recalls an American teacher disciplining a young girl at school. "Look me in the eye," the teacher insisted. But the student continued to stare at the floor. Frustrated by the girl's lack of response, the teacher sent her home with a note to her parents. The next day, the girl's mother visited the school and explained that the family was from Mexico, where it's considered impolite to look into the eyes of an authority figure. "She doesn't even look at [the eyes of] her grandparents," said her mother. "To do so would be disrespectful."

Many people from Asian, Caribbean, and Latin American cultures avoid eye contact as a sign of respect, explains Dresser. This differs greatly from the US belief that looking into people's eyes shows attentiveness and authenticity. Many urban teens, on the other hand, consider it an insult to stare directly at another person, says Dresser. They call it mad-dogging, and it's an "invitation to violence."

TO SMILE OR NOT TO SMILE

Smiling is a universal expression. But it is interpreted differently by some cultures, she says. In Japan a smile suggests silliness, so most people won't smile for photo IDs such as driver's licenses. Doing so would mean they were taking the responsibility lightly. "Until the twentieth century, some Japanese women shaved their eyebrows and blackened their teeth to veil natural expression," Dresser says. In twenty-first-century Japan, many women continue to cover their mouths when they talk or laugh.

It's all part of keeping feelings in check. This is common in cultures such as Japan, Norway, and Finland, which generally take a more socially reserved approach to relationships, says Goman. People in these countries tend to monitor their emotions and rarely express them. This contrasts with affective cultures such as Italy, Argentina, and Lebanon. There, the norm is to openly

It's not unusual for a woman in Japan to cover up a smile. In Japan, people generally aren't as free with expressions of emotion as are people in the United States and some other parts of the world.

show emotions. "In an Italian home, for example, family members may talk loudly and wave their hands more often than most others," says Goman. "They're animated and use larger gestures—something you typically wouldn't see in a Japanese home." Neither style is right or wrong, she says, they're just different.

Being aware of those differences helps prevent miscommunications—

REALITY CHECKLIST

Reading body language is more than decoding signals. "It's also about understanding how to get to the real meaning behind those signals," says Goman. A friend may look angry, but you can't tell if he's angry at you, upset because he bit his tongue, or disappointed that he lost a big game. "This is where many people make mistakes reading body language," she says. They base their interpretation on what *they* think or feel instead of what the other person may be thinking and feeling.

Our brains are wired to automatically pick up body language signals, interpret them, and instantly respond. But sometimes our first reactions lead us to wrong conclusions. Someone who seems unfriendly may simply be shy. To be as accurate as possible when reading cues, Goman says, it's important to run a reality check using the Five Cs.

1. CONTEXT: Understanding the circumstances behind behaviors is important to translating what they mean. Is a friend putting his head down and crossing his arms because he's outside and he's cold? Or is he talking with you in the hallway and acting defensively in response to something you've said? The key is to pay attention to the situation. Considering the context of your friend's behaviors—where you're talking, what's being said, when it happened—will help you decide their meaning.

at school, in the community, or with people you meet in other countries. It's impossible to know every multicultural move. But staying alert to what people are doing and taking your cues from them is a good first step, says Goman. "There's plenty of nonverbal information you can pick up on. How close does someone stand? How often does he smile? How much emotion does she show?" You may have doubts about the meaning of a

2. CLUSTERS: The best body language cues come in clusters—a group of at least three signals that support a common meaning, says Goman. When you see one nonverbal cue, such as a smile, look for two others that support it. If a person smiles, leans toward you, and lightly touches your arm, for example, her interest is likely to be genuine.

3. CONGRUENCE: How closely does a person's body language match her words? When people say what they feel, the two will usually be in sync. If not, you'll hear someone saying "Congratulations" without smiling or making eye contact. "Incongruence is a sign not so much of intentional deceit but of inner conflict between what someone is thinking and what he or she is saying," says Goman.

4. CONSISTENCY: When reading body language, it helps to have a sense of a person's normal or baseline behavior under relaxed, nonthreatening conditions. This makes it easier to spot changes. It's also one reason we're better at reading good friends and family members than strangers and acquaintances.

5. CULTURE: People's behaviors vary depending on the communities in which they live. A greeting in one country may be an insult in another. The same holds true for different parts of the country, neighborhoods, and school subcultures. Body language for students in the drama club, for example, is likely to differ from that of jocks, hip-hops, and nerds.

behavior or what to do in a particular circumstance. In those situations, ask for help. "If your heart is in the right place—if you really want to learn about people and their culture, most will be happy to show you the way," explains Goman.

TAKE ACTION!

The next time you're at a family gathering or eating at a friend's house, notice how people interact. Who makes big hand gestures? Who's off to the side, quietly talking one-on-one? Are people smiling and making eye contact? To learn more, start by asking a few people about their family's style of communication. Is it expressive or reserved? Do they come from a cultural background that might explain their body language?

Amy Cuddy learned to fake the courage of cartoon superheros *(right)* as part of her recovery from a brain injury. It's a skill she still uses and shares with others. Cuddy specializes in research about the link between human body language and behavior.

6

FAKE IT . . . UNTIL YOU BECOME IT

Amy Cuddy always thought of herself as smart. Until the accident. That's when the nineteen-year-old college sophomore found herself in a hospital with a severe head injury. The car that she'd been riding in with friends crashed at 90 miles (145 kilometers) per hour. Not only did Cuddy fly out of the vehicle, she also rolled several times after hitting the ground. Scarier yet, tests at the hospital showed a significant drop in her IQ. Doctors told her she could do many things when she was released from the hospital, but finishing college was probably not one of them.

Cuddy was devastated. Her whole identity had been wrapped around being smart—even gifted. Now what? "I felt entirely powerless," she says. After the initial shock, a determined Cuddy struggled back. She studied passionately each day until she regained her skills. Eventually she graduated from college and later was accepted to graduate school at Princeton University in New Jersey.

Even with her amazing success, Cuddy questioned her abilities. She wondered if she really belonged at Princeton. At the end of her first year there, she had to give a twenty-minute talk. But she felt like such a phony, she almost dropped out of school instead. "I was so afraid of being found out," she says. Her advisor wouldn't let her quit. She insisted that Cuddy "fake it" for this talk and all others until she felt confident and comfortable with herself and her skills.

The tough love worked. It pushed Cuddy all the way through to her first year of teaching at Harvard University in Massachusetts. By then, most of her early fears had faded. At the end of one semester, a quiet student who hadn't said a word in Cuddy's class showed up at her office. She was worried about failing the course for lack of participation. "I'm not supposed to be here," the student said, echoing Cuddy's earlier feelings about herself. "You are supposed to be here!" answered Cuddy. "And tomorrow you're going to fake it. . . . You're going to go into the classroom, and you're going to give the best [class] comment ever." And she did.

POWER MOVES

Cuddy didn't realize it on her road to recovery, but her experience became a prime example of how we can use our bodies to change our minds. Now she has the research to prove it. Many studies show that body language affects how *other* people view us. But Cuddy and two professors from Columbia University in New York have also verified that our actions influence how *we* see ourselves.

Want to feel more confident and **powerful** before giving a book report or taking that math test? Run to the bathroom and stand like a superhero in front of a mirror. Cuddy's research shows that people who spend two minutes striking a power pose—such as standing with their hands on their hips and their legs about 6 inches (15 centimeters) apart—feel more self-assured. Standing in expansive poses, such as the superhero stance, changes our blood chemistry. When we act as if we're powerful, our levels of testosterone—the hormone linked with power and energy—increase. Our levels of cortisol—the stress hormone—drop. This helps us walk a little taller and behave more assertively when we're meeting new people or performing in front of an audience. On the other hand, when our bodies curl up and constrict, our stress hormones rise and our power hormones fall. This mix makes it more difficult to adapt to social situations we might find scary.

Try out the superhero power pose like these two girls to boost your confidence. Research shows this trick actually helps you perform better in front of a crowd!

TAIL-WAGGING

A common challenge we face during interviews, auditions, and tryouts is showing off our true potential. One behavior that can spoil our efforts is tail-wagging, says Cara Hale Alter. Just as dogs wag their tails to signal that they're friendly and nonthreatening, so do people. The only difference is that human tail-wagging looks more like "a flash of a smile, a dip of the chin," hands in pockets, and all-round "aw shucks" behavior, she explains. It's an automatic body language that fosters friendships. However, it doesn't work as well in situations where people are judging our skills. They want to see our genuine strengths, says Alter. They aren't interested in behaviors that say, "Please take it easy on me. I'm really uncomfortable on the spot." Tail-wagging behaviors may persuade people to back off during an interview, she says. But they can also cost you the position you're seeking.

The solution? "Strong posture, strong voice, and strong eye contact."

PLAYING THE PART

"We can look comfortable far sooner than we can feel it," says Cara Hale Alter, author of *The Credibility Code: How to Project Confidence & Competence When It Matters Most*. The racing heart and foggy thinking that sometimes go along with stressful situations feel uncomfortable. Yet 90 percent of those symptoms aren't visible, she explains. "People can't see your heart beating." What they can see, however, is our body language—and that's something we can control. Instead of giving in to our first reactions, which may tell us to shrink or freeze, we can take on a posture of confidence. This will make us *look* and *feel* more comfortable.

In Western cultures, creating a strong presence starts with three essential behaviors, says Alter. The first is having strong posture—keeping your spine straight, your shoulders pulled back, and your head level. Lowering your chin can make you look shy when you're speaking. Raising it can look arrogant, and tilting it can make you seem unsure, she says. By standing tall and being level headed, "you'll look more dynamic, more focused, and more purposeful."

The second key is to speak with a strong voice. Aim for a voice that is above average in volume and doesn't trail off at the end of sentences. The stronger the volume, the more confident you'll appear, says Alter. "It's no mystery: It takes a strong body to produce a strong voice, which is one reason people with strong voices are perceived as more powerful."

The third way to project confidence is by making and maintaining eye contact. When speaking to a group, the ideal length of eye contact is three to five seconds per person, Alter says. This shows that you

Standing tall and straight, making eye contact with your listeners, and speaking in a confident voice are key to making a good presentation in front of a group.

view "listeners as individuals, visually connecting with each one for a short time as if it were a one-on-one conversation."

Using these skills and making them a habit is the key to building a strong presence, says Alter. This becomes especially important when you're meeting people for the first time—whether it's at a band audition, team tryouts, or a job interview.

TAKE ACTION!

When talking in front of an audience, try these steps for success.

- Before you start, power pose for two minutes to build confidence.
- Take a few deep belly breaths and slowly count to six as you inhale and exhale.
- Walk on stage with good posture, standing tall and holding your head level. Smile and look around the room.
- Maintain steady eye contact with the audience throughout the talk. Look at individuals in the audience and hold your gaze for three to five seconds per person.
- Speak with a strong, expressive voice.
- Talk with your hands, using gestures to highlight important ideas and to express emotions.
- Move when you can to keep the audience engaged. Walk toward people when making a key point and step back when you're changing subjects.
- Smile big and thank your audience when you're done. You did it!

"You only have seven seconds to make a first impression," says Goman. In that time, people decide whether you're likable, smart, trustworthy, friendly, believable, and competent. People may change those feelings as they get to know you. But first impressions—which are mostly based on nonverbal cues—can be hard to shake. "This is why you need to align your body with as many positive signals as possible," says Goman. "It makes a difference whether you walk into a room smiling or frowning. It affects how people perceive you—and how you feel about yourself."

SOURCE NOTES

5 Reuters, "Town Seeks Ban on Political Smirks," *CNN.com*, April 8, 2003, http://www .cnn.com/2003/ALLPOLITICS/04/08/smirk.ban.reut/index.html.

6 Carol Kinsey Goman, telephone conversation with Donna Jackson, December 22, 2012.

8 Ibid.

9 Ibid.

9 Joe Navarro, "The Key to Understanding Body Language," *PsychologyToday.com*, October 28, 2009, http://www.psychologytoday.com/blog/spycatcher/200910 /the-key-understanding-body-language.

10 Carol Kinsey Goman, e-mail to Donna Jackson, August 26, 2013.

13 Daniel McNeill, *The Face* (Boston: Little, Brown, 1998), 22.

13 Ibid.

13 Goman, telephone conversation with Donna Jackson, December 22, 2012.

13–14 "Basketball Intangibles: The Power of Eyes," YouTube video, 3:51, posted by PGCschape, January 23, 2012, http://www.youtube.com/watch?v=SnT33VXe_ls.

16 Carol Kinsey Goman, telephone conversation with Donna Jackson, January 15, 2013.

16 Ibid.

18 Maureen Grier, telephone conversation with Donna Jackson, April 8, 2013.

18 Klutz, *How to Draw Funny: Give Your Doodles a Comic Twist,* with the assistance of David Sheldon (Palo Alto, CA: Klutz, 2009), 13.

19 Goman, telephone conversation with Donna Jackson, January 15, 2013.

20 Ibid.

21 Ibid.

21 Goman, telephone conversation with Donna Jackson, December 22, 2012.

25 Ibid.

27 Benedict Carey, "Evidence That Little Touches Do Mean So Much," *New York Times*, February 23, 2010, http://www.nytimes.com/2010/02/23/health/23mind.html?_r=0.

27 Goman, telephone conversation with Donna Jackson, January 15, 2013.

28 Ibid.

29 Carol Kinsey Goman, e-mail to Donna Jackson, August 21, 2013.

31 Philip Houston, Michel Floyd, Susan Carnicero, and Don Tennant, *Spy the Lie* (New York: St. Martin's Press, 2012), 15.

31 Daniel Strain, "Why Creepy People Give Us the Chills," *Science*, April 23, 2012, http://news.sciencemag.org/2012/04/why-creepy-people-give-us-chills.

31 Carol Kinsey Goman, telephone conversation with Donna Jackson, January 2, 2013.

33 Ibid.

33–34 Ibid.

36 "Dr. Cynthia Breazeal—Part 1—the Personal Side of Robots," YouTube video, 31:12, posted by DSEvideo, December 4, 2009, http://www.youtube.com/watch?v=s3MJ5BU3C20.

37 Robert H. Frank, quoted in Tara Parker-Pope, "Who's Trustworthy? A Robot Can Help Teach Us," *New York Times*, September 10, 2012, http://well.blogs.nytimes.com/2012/09/10/whos-trustworthy-a-robot-can-help-teach-us.

38–39 Kalista Consol, personal communications with Donna Jackson, December 26, 2012; February 13, 2013.

39 Ibid.

40 Ibid.

40–41 Carol Kinsey Goman, telephone conversation with Donna Jackson, February 20, 2013.

42 Consol, personal communications with Donna Jackson, December 26, 2012; February 13, 2013.

42 Norine Dresser, telephone conversation with Donna Jackson, May 25, 2012.

42 Ibid.

43 Ibid.

43   Norine Dresser, *Multicultural Manners: Essential Rules of Etiquette for the 21st Century*, rev. ed., (Hoboken, NJ: John Wiley & Sons, 2005), 21.

44   Goman, telephone conversation with Donna Jackson, February 20, 2013.

44   Carol Kinsey Goman, *The Nonverbal Advantage: Secrets and Science of Body Language at Work* (San Francisco: Berrett-Koehler Publishers, 2008), 19.

44   Goman, telephone conversation with Donna Jackson, December 22, 2012.

45   Goman, *The Nonverbal Advantage*, 16.

45–46   Ibid.

47   Amy Cuddy, "Amy Cuddy: Your Body Language Shapes Who You Are," TEDGlobal, filmed June 2012, posted October 2012, http://www.ted.com/talks/amy_cuddy_your_body_language_shapes_who_you_are.html.

48   Ibid.

48   Ibid.

48   Ibid.

50   Cara Hale Alter, *The Credibility Code: How to Project Confidence & Competence When It Matters Most* (San Francisco: Meritus Books, 2012), 98.

50   Ibid., 96.

50   Cara Hale Alter, telephone conversation with Donna Jackson, March 20, 2013.

50   Ibid.

50   Ibid.

51   Alter, *The Credibility Code*, 17.

51   Ibid., 48.

52   Ibid., 69.

53   Goman, telephone conversation with Donna Jackson, December 22, 2012.

53   Ibid.

BODY TALK GLOSSARY

baseline: a person's normal behavior under relaxed conditions

body language: nonverbal communication expressed consciously and unconsciously through actions such as gestures, eye contact, posture, touching, proximity, and facial expressions

devil's horns: overall negative feelings about someone, based on a negative characteristic and/or how much we dislike that person

Duper's Delight: a fleeting smile after a lie, indicating that a person (the liar) believes he or she has fooled someone

eye contact: looking directly into someone's eyes. It is viewed as a sign of an honest, interested person.

facial expressions: feelings conveyed through a person's face. Seven expressions are considered universal: anger, happiness, disgust, surprise, fear, sadness, and contempt.

fidgeting: nervous or impatient movements that are often quick and repeated. They typically indicate that a person is nervous, uncomfortable, or bored.

first impression: the immediate feeling you have about a person, based mostly on body language

gesture cluster: a group of movements, postures, and actions that reinforce a common meaning

gestures: body movements that express or emphasize thoughts, ideas, and emotions

halo effect: overall positive feelings about a person, based on a positive characteristic and/or how much we like or love that person

innate: present from birth

kinesics: the study of body movements and their role in communication

limbic system: the part of the brain that is the first to receive emotional information and to react to it

microexpressions: fleeting facial expressions that last less than one-fifth of a second and reveal emotions people are trying to conceal

mirroring: mimicking the body language of others—either consciously or unconsciously—as a way of saying that we like or agree with them

nonverbal communication: messages sent without using words. These include gestures, facial expressions, body posture, and proximity.

pacifying gestures: self-touching gestures, such as rubbing the arms or legs. These gestures calm and comfort us during stressful situations.

proxemics: the study of how people use personal space, such as the distance we stand from someone when talking, and what it means

tail-wagging: body language, such as a shy smile, that tells others you're friendly and not a threat

true smile: a smile of enjoyment that engages the muscles of the mouth and the eyes

turtle effect: a body language display where the shoulders move up toward the ears as if someone is burying the head like a turtle. It shows lack of confidence.

vocal cues: voice qualities, such as tone, rate, pitch, and volume, that reveal our emotions and can change the meaning of our message

SELECTED BIBLIOGRAPHY

Alter, Cara Hale. *The Credibility Code: How to Project Confidence & Competence When It Matters Most.* San Francisco: Meritus Books, 2012.

Armstrong, Nancy, and Melissa Wagner. *Field Guide to Gestures: How to Identify and Interpret Virtually Every Gesture Known to Man.* Philadelphia: Quirk Books, 2003.

Bates, Brian. *The Human Face.* With the assistance of John Cleese. London: Dorling Kindersley, 2001.

Dresser, Norine. *Multicultural Manners: Essential Rules of Etiquette for the 21st Century.* Rev. ed. Hoboken, NJ: John Wiley & Sons, 2005.

Driver, Janine. *You Say More Than You Think.* New York: Crown Publishers, 2010.

Ekman, Paul. *Emotions Revealed: Recognizing Faces and Feelings to Improve Communication and Emotional Life.* New York: St. Martin's Press, 2007.

———. *Telling Lies: Clues to Deceit in the Marketplace, Politics, and Marriage.* New York: W. W. Norton, 2009.

Goman, Carol Kinsey. *The Nonverbal Advantage: Secrets and Science of Body Language at Work.* San Francisco: Berrett-Koehler Publishers, 2008.

———. *The Silent Language of Leaders.* San Francisco: Jossey-Bass, 2011.

Houston, Philip, Michel Floyd, Susan Carnicero, and Don Tennant. *Spy the Lie.* New York: St. Martin's Press, 2012.

McNeill, Daniel. *The Face.* Boston: Little, Brown, 1998.

Navarro, Joe. *What Every Body Is Saying.* With the assistance of Marvin Karlins. New York: HarperCollins, 2008.

Pease, Allan, and Barbara Pease. *The Definitive Book of Body Language.* New York: Bantam Dell, 2006.

EXPLORE MORE!

BOOKS

Briggs, Nadine, and Donna Shea. *How to Make & Keep Friends: Tips for Kids to Overcome 50 Common Social Challenges.* Seattle: CreateSpace, 2011.

Canfield, Jack, and Kent Healy. *The Success Principles for Teens: How to Get from Where You Are to Where You Want to Be.* Deerfield Beach, FL: Health Communications, 2008.

Ceceri, Kathy. *Robotics: Discover the Science and Technology of the Future with 20 Projects.* Build It Yourself series. White River Junction, VT: Nomad Press, 2012.

Fox, Marci G., and Leslie Sokol. *Think Confident, Be Confident for Teens.* Oakland: Instant Help Books, 2011.

Jackson, Donna M. *In Your Face: The Facts about Your Features.* New York: Viking, 2004.

Klutz. *How to Draw Funny: Give Your Doodles a Comic Twist.* With the assistance of David Sheldon. Palo Alto, CA: Klutz, 2009.

Wolfe, Gillian. *LOOK! Body Language in Art.* London: Frances Lincoln Children's Books, 2004.

WEB VIDEOS

Carol Kinsey Goman

http://www.CKG.com

Check out Goman's site for short videos about body language.

My Science Academy—the Science of Lying

http://myscienceacademy.org/2013/04/25/the-science-of-lying/

Discover why we lie and how a pathological liar's brain differs from yours.

NBC News—the Ghanaian Handshake

http://www.nbcnews.com/video/nightly-news/31804849#31804849

See the Ghanaian handshake in action.

Science of Attraction—the Halo Effect

http://www.scienceofattraction.co.uk/factoids/halo-effect

Do we ignore negative qualities in a person based on positive ones? Watch this experiment and find out.

TED Talks—Amy Cuddy: Your Body Language Shapes Who You Are

http://www.ted.com/talks/amy_cuddy_your_body_language_shapes_who_you_are.html

Hear social psychologist Amy Cuddy's inspiring talk about power posing.

LERNER

SOURCE™

Expand learning beyond the printed book. Download free, complementary educational resources for this book from our website, www.lernerresource.com.

INDEX

ABOUT THE AUTHORS

Donna M. Jackson is an award-winning author of nonfiction books for young readers. Her works include the critically acclaimed *Elephant Scientist*, named a 2012 Robert F. Sibert honor book, a 2012 *Boston Globe–Horn Book* nonfiction honor book, and an NSTA/CBC Outstanding Science Trade book; *Extreme Scientists,* selected as a 2009 Smithsonian Notable Book for Children; and *ER Vets,* an Orbis Pictus and ASPCA Henry Bergh honor book. Donna's interest in the mind-body connection began when she first studied psychology in college. Later, while writing a book called *In Your Face*, she became fascinated with facial expressions and the many messages we communicate through body language—both to ourselves and others. Donna holds a master's degree in journalism from the University of Colorado at Boulder. She lives near the Rocky Mountains with her husband, Charlie, their family, and their two dogs, Shadow and Sydney.

Carol Kinsey Goman, PhD, is a body-language expert who gives speeches and seminars around the world. She is the author of two body language books for people in the workplace: *The Nonverbal Advantage* and *The Silent Language of Leaders*. She and her husband, Ray, live in Berkeley, California, with their adorable, and spoiled, Cavalier King Charles spaniel, Lord Nelson.

PHOTO ACKNOWLEDGMENTS

The images in this book are used with the permission of: © iStockphoto.com/Izabela Habur, p. 4; © Laura Westlund/Independent Picture Service, pp. 6, 26, 32; © Andrew Rich/Vetta/ Getty Images, p. 7; © Leigh Schindler/E+/Getty Images, p. 8; © iStockphoto/Thinkstock, p. 10; © Sam Edwards/OJO+/Getty Images, p. 12; © Michael Dwyer/Alamy, p. 14; © Nicole Hill Gerulat/Getty Images, p. 15; © Digital Vision/Thinkstock, p. 17; © iStockphoto.com/Brett Lamb, p. 18; © Kondoros Éva Katalin/E+/Getty Images, p. 21; © Todor Tsvetkov/E+/Getty Images, p. 22; © Photodisc/Getty Images, p. 24; © Jonathan Daniel/Getty Images, p. 27; © Comstock/ Thinkstock, p. 28; © Laurence Mouton/PhotoAlto/Getty Images, p. 30; © JGI/Jamie Grill/ Blend Images/Getty Images, p. 34; © David L Ryan/Boston Globe/Getty Images, p. 36; Sjantani Chatterjee/Reuters/Newscom, p. 37; © Kim Steele/Blend Images/Alamy, p. 38; © Easy Track Ghana, p. 39; © iStockphoto.com/MariaPavlova, p. 41; © RunPhoto/The Image Bank/Getty Images, p. 43; © iStockphoto.com/VasjaKoman, p. 47; © Franek Strzeszewski/Image Source/ Alamy, p. 49; © Uwe Umstatter/Alamy, p. 51.
Front cover: © Pixattitude/Dreamstime.com (headstand); © Photoeuphoria/Dreamstime.com (woman walking); © Pixattitude/Dreamstime.com (young man).

Main body text set in Avenir LT Pro 45 Book 14/22. Typeface provided by Linotype AG.